TIME FOR KIDS READERS

garden of DREAMS

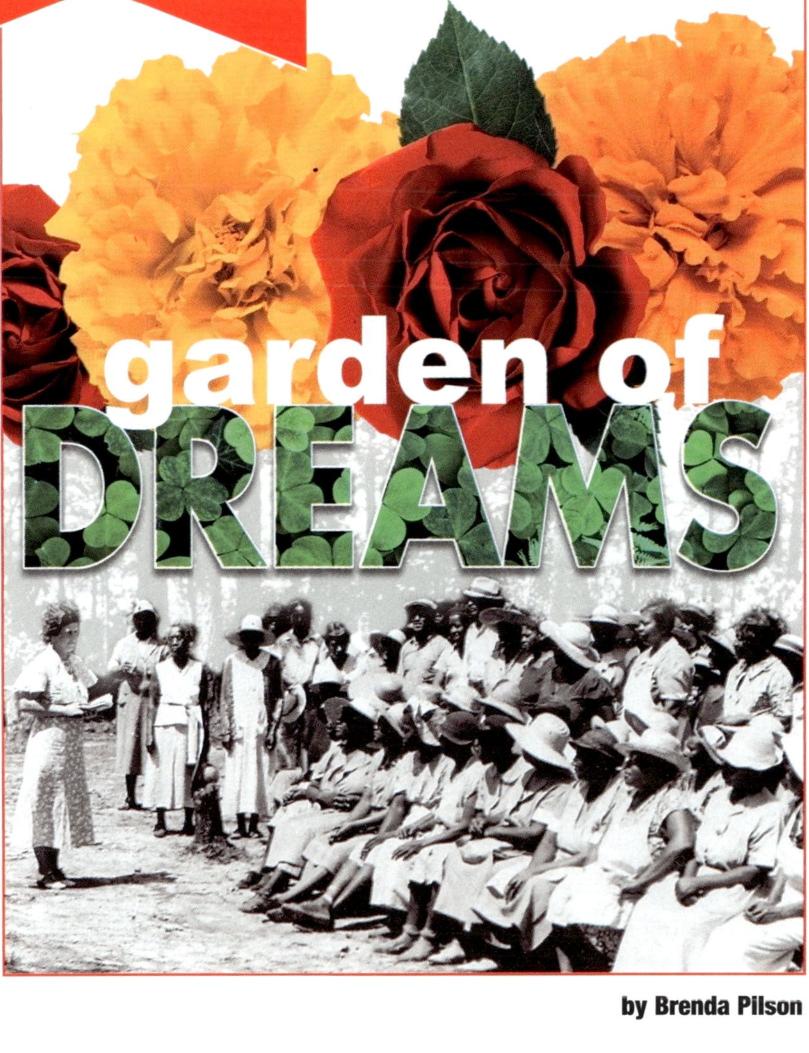

by Brenda Pilson

Harcourt
Orlando Austin Chicago New York Toronto London San Diego

Visit *The Learning Site!*
www.harcourtschool.com

"On 25 acres of land dwelled a prickly, green wilderness. It was a sea of trees, trees, and more trees!" That's how a densely wooded piece of property in Norfolk, Virginia, was described in 1936. Although it may have lacked beauty, the land certainly did not lack possibilities. At least that's what Thomas Thompson, the city manager of Norfolk, Virginia, thought. Norfolk had few parks. Thompson wanted to change that. He wanted to fix up this corner of his city. But how could that be done?

Thomas Thompson saw this woodland area and knew it could be the start of a wonderful garden.

Flowers! That's what Thompson had in mind. He dreamed of turning the land into a flourishing garden, a kind of plant museum. It would become a special spot for local residents. It would attract tourists from across the country. "This new garden would be the Venice of the United States!" he said.

Charles Gillette

Thompson asked Charles Gillette of Virginia, known for his landscape designs, to plan the garden. Gillette suggested Frederic Heutte (HYOO•it), who studied flowers and plants, as the city's landscape supervisor.

Thompson, Gillette, and Heutte had great hopes for this new project. There was one big problem, though. Where would they get the money to develop the land? The United States was in the middle of the Great Depression. Jobs were scarce and money was more so.

The Works Progress Administration (WPA), a government program, came to the rescue. President Franklin D. Roosevelt had started it in 1935. One of its goals was to create jobs for the many people who were out of work. On June 30, 1939, the United States government approved $76,278 toward what became known as the *Azalea Garden Project*. Now Norfolk had the money to begin work. All that was needed were people who were willing to do the work.

The Four Seasons Garden (left) is used as an outdoor classroom. Here, students can see 50 different kinds of wildflowers and the birds and insects they attract.

Super Women

Not far from the garden site, groups of African American women made their living in the heat of the sweltering sun. They grew spinach, cabbage, beans, and other vegetables on small farms. Because of the hard times, these jobs were disappearing. The women needed another way to earn money. The WPA had an idea.

On September 15, 1938, the WPA hired nearly 200 African American women to begin work on the Azalea Garden Project. The women spent every day digging up roots and pushing heavy wheelbarrows filled with soil. They cleared the thick vegetation by using tools such as hoes, shovels, rakes, and pitchforks. These same tools were used to kill the poisonous snakes that sometimes made an appearance. One worker, Josephine Rollins, killed eight such snakes in one day!

azaleas

The women planted:
- 4,000 azaleas
- 2,000 rhododendrons
- 100 bushels of daffodils
- several thousand shrubs and trees

These women worked in the garden from the start of the project. In this photo, they're preparing mulch, or ground covering, for azaleas.

About 20 men also worked on the land, but women were the lead workers. Most of the men were in charge of sharpening tools. The rest were assigned to other projects. Many Norfolk residents protested about using women to do such heavy, exhausting labor. Times were hard, however, and the women said they appreciated the chance to work. Best of all, they loved plants! After the gardens were open to the public, some of the women continued to work there.

The women worked 40 hours a week. They earned in one week what skilled garden workers today sometimes earn in one hour. By the spring of 1939, the workers had cleared about 25 acres of land, along with one mile of walking trails. They had planted several acres of flower beds.

Through the hard work and dedication of its workers, Norfolk's new Azalea Garden was well under way! In 1939, the garden opened to the public. Nothing could stand in the way of the garden's success … or so the planners thought.

daffodils

rhododendrons

The War Casts a Shadow

In 1939 World War II broke out in Europe. The WPA program was on the decline. Funds for keeping up the garden were running out fast. Many people, including Frederic Heutte, thought the garden would become a victim of the war. But the garden was saved once again by the WPA, which issued $138,553, saying this was the final payment. The funds supported the garden until 1941, when the U.S. entered the war. This money also allowed the garden to "grow." By 1941 the site had expanded from 25 to 75 acres and contained 50,000 plants.

When the WPA money was spent, the city of Norfolk had to pay the expenses. When the city's funds became low, Frederic Heutte turned to Colonel Charles B. Borland for help. Borland had replaced Thomas Thompson as Norfolk's city manager. Borland felt that the city's extra money should go to the war effort. He didn't agree that Norfolk needed to improve its tourist business, so he would grant Heutte only $5,000 a year to run the garden. That was not nearly enough to support the staff and the upkeep of the grounds. The garden was in serious danger of being closed. Heutte was not about to let that happen. He, along with the citizens of Norfolk, went to bat for their pride and joy. They were determined to save it. Enough money was donated to allow the garden to stay open.

Norfolk officials get together at the retirement of Colonel Charles B. Borland (second from right).

Finding funds to keep up the garden wasn't the only struggle. The land needed to be protected. During a routine check one morning, Heutte discovered several trucks, bulldozers, and soldiers hard at work chopping down trees! The sergeant in charge told Heutte that a section of azalea beds was being replaced by barracks for 500 U.S. Army Air Force troops. It was to be used for the rest of the war, however long that would be. By this time, the Army Air Force had already taken over the nearby airport, as well as other neighboring property. However, a colonel from Boston, who was also a flower lover, saved the day! The colonel convinced military officials that the trees would be perfect for hiding the barracks! He ordered that the garden be respected as much as possible.

In 1940, a U.S. Army Air Force plane sits near the garden.

TFK DID YOU KNOW

One hundred years ago, people in England sent secret messages by using flowers. Here are some popular blooms and their secret meanings.

FLOWER	MESSAGE
Baby's Breath	Pure of Heart
Daisy	Hope, Innocence
Ivy	Marriage
Lavender	Undying Love
Lily-of-the-Valley	Peace
Rose	Love
Violet	Faithfulness

TFK FAST FACTS

- More than 250,000 people participate in and attend the seven-day Azalea Festival each year during the third week in April. The festival earns about one million dollars, which benefits many Norfolk businesses.
- The garden is cared for by 15 gardeners and groundskeepers. About 120 volunteers also care for the grounds.

U.S. President Lyndon B. Johnson crowns his daughter, Luci Baines, queen of the Azalea Festival. Being crowned queen is considered a great honor.

How the Garden Grew

After the war was over, nothing was allowed to stand in the garden's way. Major Frank Turin, a Norfolk official, believed the garden could become a big tourist attraction. With his help, the garden got lots of much-needed publicity in 1947. This was good news for everyone involved!

Of course, more fame meant more tourists. In 1947, as a way to raise money, visitors were charged an entrance fee of 25 cents for each car. The money was used for putting up new buildings and adding or improving roads. The city was also able to buy more land, enlarging the garden to 250 acres. This led to major collections of azaleas, rhododendrons, camellias, hollies, dogwoods, crape myrtles, flowering fruit trees, annuals, and more flowers.

To add to the garden's growing importance, in 1953 it became the site for the annual International Azalea Festival.

In 1967, gardeners planted areas around the canal (above), which is shaped like a "Y." Today, visitors enjoy the flowers while taking a half-hour boat ride on the canal (below). The garden is said to be the only one in the U.S. that can be toured by both boat and tram.

A Time of Change

From 1958 to 1963, the garden went through a lot of changes. Canals were dug so boat tours could float through. Trams, or trackless trains, were built to carry visitors throughout the garden. In 1971, nearby Norfolk International Airport was expanded. As a result, the garden needed to sell some land to the airport. Although this action reduced the garden from 250 to 155 acres, the airport brought in more tourists. In 1976—on the 200th birthday of the United States—the Bicentennial Rose Garden was dedicated. In the mid-1980s, the garden officially became the Norfolk Botanical Garden.

TFK

Top 3 Blooms at the Norfolk Botanical Garden

1. More than 200,000 **azaleas** blossom from mid-April through May.
2. The **rose** garden has more than 300,000 blooms in May and October.
3. The **camellia** is a winter-blooming plant that perks up the garden during the colder months.

This flower-filled wooded area, part of the original garden, is reflected in Mirror Lake.

Surrounded by Lake Whitehurst, the Norfolk Botanical Garden today offers visitors 12 miles (19 km) of winding trails and landscaped canals. It has one of the largest and most diverse collections of azaleas, camellias, rhododendrons, and roses on the East Coast.

Few, if any, people who visit the garden today realize what it looked like in 1938. Today, however, the men and women who worked to create the Norfolk Botanical Garden would see it as proof that dreams really can come true.

A meadow shows visitors that wildflowers and grasses are as pleasing and interesting as flowers in a formal, planned garden.

TFK FAST FACTS

FLOWER GLOSSARY

Annuals: flowers that grow and bloom for just one season

Biennials: flowers that need two growing seasons to bloom

Perennials: flowers that bloom year after year

4 GOLDEN RULES OF GARDENING

If you're thinking of starting your own garden, here are some tips to help you develop your green thumb!

1. Start with good soil. You can make homemade compost out of fallen leaves and dead plants. This will attract earthworms, which will work the organic matter into your soil and keep it healthy.

2. Think about your garden. Find flowers and trees that grow naturally where you live, instead of plants from faraway places. Choose plants that will grow well in your garden's present condition. Plants grow best in gardens where they get enough sunlight, nutrients, and water.

3. Welcome nature's creatures. Bees, ladybugs, and birds will help your garden grow by protecting it from bugs that could destroy your plants. Make sure you grow plants that these creatures enjoy!

4. Create a garden that you can call your own. Grow plants that interest you and that are easy for you to work with. Best of all, have fun!

* Adapted from *The Kids Can Press Jumbo Book of Gardening*, 2000

At the Norfolk Botanical Gardens, a Japanese garden honors Kitakyushu (kee•TAH•kyoo•shoo), Norfolk's sister city.